RISE ABOVE
ADVERSITY

Where Declaration Becomes Destiny

CHRISTINA CRUZ-MENDEZ
JusChrist4

RISE ABOVE ADVERSITY

Copyright © Christina Cruz-Mendez 2018
ISBN: 978-1-9164444-9-2

Published and Printed by:
Gracehouse Publishing
56, Gosport Road, Walthamstow,
London, United Kingdom, E17 7LY

Unless otherwise indicated, all Scripture quotations are taken from the King James Version (KJV) of the Bible.

All rights reserved.
No portion of this book may be used
 without the written permission of the
 publisher, with the exception of brief
 excerpts in magazines, articles, reviews, etc.

Contents

DEDICATION	| 05
FOREWORD	| 09
INTRODUCTION	| 13
CHAPTER 1: Anthony: Our Gladiator	| 19
CHAPTER 2: RISE above adversity	| 25
CHAPTER 3: Recalibrating	| 35
CHAPTER 4: Over and Over Again	| 43
CHAPTER 5: Every Time	| 49
CHAPTER 6: Bullet Points	| 53
CHAPTER 7: Discarding Negative Thoughts	| 61
CHAPTER 8: When Good Things Are Negative	| 67

CHAPTER 9:
When Nothing Works | 71

CHAPTER 10:
Times Like This | 77

CHAPTER 11:
His Might Against Our Might | 83

CHAPTER 12:
The Walk | 87

CHAPTER 13:
Be Grateful, Thankful | 97

CHAPTER 14:
40 Days Left | 101

CHAPTER 15:
Condition the Mind for Greatness | 107

CHAPTER 16:
Atmosphere Changer | 117

CHAPTER 17:
Because Of Our Chains | 125

BIOGRAPHY | 131

DEDICATION

To Juan Antonio, My love. My beloved husband, in all my life I would never wish to see your pained face like this again. I never want to see light leave you ever again. I never want to be in that place to tell you the worst. May God give you so much inside that the emptiness you feel is immediately replenished by His grace. You give all that you have in you to rise each day into the God-given position that He has called you. You define what it is to rise each day. You walk it, breathe it and live it. You are my hero.

To Cristina, I am so sorry my covenant sister. If I could swallow your pain in an instant I would. It hurts me to see you like this. It hurts me that you have to go through this. It just hurts so badly.

I love you so much. Because you are an amazing person. You really are.

Ezekiel, Isaiah and Ezrabella.... May God grant you great grace and understanding in due season. May all of us do more to help stand in an irreplaceable gap somehow and some way. You all are the epitome of what it is to rise above adversity.

Pastor Nelly, I am so sorry that I missed the mark in this. I hate to know that the one thing you loved most was stripped from you in a moment. Joy left your heart and a deep companion that made up for everything that lacked with earthly connections. And as you stand to face your own health battles I know that you will continue to teach me every day how to rise.

Cassandra Isabella & Samuel Isaiah! I hated telling you somehow that someone so valuable was removed from our family suddenly and so tragically. Humanity hit us. You both rose up.

Yarina, it was so difficult to sit across from you and see you in so much pain. You were withering away in that moment into the darkest place of your life and taught us how to rise. Not only that but you kicked adversity in the face with your faith, persistence and love for life. You are what I call BRAVE.

To the family, churches, spiritual sons and daughters, partners, and friends that pass through your own adversity. You teach me new things by your courage. Don't stop now... you got this far with God.

God is sovereign and will show us things that go beyond what our natural comprehension could ever.

Lastly and most importantly, Antonio Juan Mendez.... your

07 / Dedication

dedication is by itself an opening to these intimate chapters. You have always and will always be that great and effective door for us all. We will roar together and continue to rise so we can finish this race.

#MendezStrong

Love you always!!!!
Yoooooooooooooooooooooooo

"Until we understand who we are and why we were created, we won't understand why we go through what we go through." – Pastor Tony Mendez
Heaven on Earth International Church
10/8/82 – 4/2/17

RISE ABOVE ADVERSITY / 08 ◆◆◆

FOREWORD

RISE ABOVE ADVERSITY! Isn't it interesting that most Christians refer to themselves as an overcomer in Christ Jesus? Well, this statement is true because the scriptures state it on more than one occasion that through Jesus Christ we will overcome trials and tribulations. (1 John 4:4, 1 John 5:4).

However, I do not think for a moment that such connotation would be made without the possibilities of facing challenges or obstacles as a child of God because to so many Christians, this doesn't make any sense hence the question "why?". Reasons because as a child of a loving God His children should never go through any form of tribulation. Unfortunately, it is not so; what the word of God promises is that when believers go through adversity; through the unfailing love and grace of God they will rise above it.

In Psalm 34, it is clearly stated that many will be the afflictions of the righteous, but the Lord will deliver them from all; meaning that a believer should not be caught unaware or be completely overwhelmed when adversity comes otherwise it will be needless to be referred to as an overcomer in Christ

Again, in the gospel we see Jesus encouraging his disciples and his followers saying to them that as long as they are in this world, trials and tribulations are inevitable. But he encouraged them not to worry because through Him they will overcome each and every storm that comes their way. Glory to Jesus!

The truth is this; no book can completely answer the questions many Christians who have had to endure difficult times have been asking for many decades because only God holds answers to these questions. However, what many great authors including Pastor Christina have exegetically written is to help bring some form of healing, comfort as well as guidance through God's word and personal stories on how to rise above the storms of adversity.

As I read through this book, I couldn't help but think about Joseph in the Bible who unknowingly made a 'grave' mistake sharing his dreams with his brothers and to his dismay, he watched how his brothers did everything possible to stop his dream from becoming a reality.

In very similar ways, adversities are like Joseph's brothers; people who are vicious dream killers that will come at you in several ways but their evil intentions still will not be able to change God's plans about you. This is why you and I must refuse to give up when we are faced with adversities in our lives because the truth is that we actually advance in times of adversities as we see in the story of Joseph (Genesis 37–41).

Just like yesterday, I remember the passing of my mother, a woman who passionately loved and served the Lord but died at the age of 62 years to cancer. I was in total despair as I found her lifeless on the bed the morning after we had only just celebrated my daughter's birthday. A thousand and one questions raced through my mind. I asked why would a God-fearing and God-loving woman's life end in such devastation? Nevertheless, I remain comforted by the word of the Lord through the Apostle Paul in 1 Corinthians 15:51-57;

"Behold! I tell you a mystery. We shall not all sleep, but we shall all be changed, in a moment, in the twinkling of an eye, at the last trumpet. For the trumpet will sound, and the dead will be raised imperishable, and we shall be changed. For this perishable body must put on the imperishable, and this mortal body must put on immortality. When the perishable puts on the imperishable, and the mortal puts on immortality, then shall come to pass the saying that is written: "Death is swallowed up in victory." "O death, where is your victory? O death, where is your sting?"

I am truly convinced that Pastor Christina Cruz-Mendez has again like she did with her last book 'Rebuilt' placed a much needed, timely and inspirational book in our hands. A book I consider a tool that will help many of us including her own family who is still healing from the tragic passing of Pastor Tony Mendez (her brother-in-law) who died in a car crash, to daily rise above our adversities.

Thank you, Pastor Christina, I pray this book gets into the hands of grieving individuals and families across the nations of the earth in Jesus name, Amen!

Apostle Femi Adun
President, *Eagle World Outreach UK*

INTRODUCTION

Have you ever thought to write a book for someone else? For those that you are so close to and intertwined to their pain that you could ALMOST hear their thoughts, feel their pain and drown in their uncontrollable sadness.

I wonder how much more Jesus was agonizing as He was familiar with our grief. So we have His word as a guide.

Oh what a situation to be rebuilt then wrecked again. To rise and to fall again. How so? Just by life! By sudden loss. By experiencing your own pain coupled with that of others so close to you. These are things that happen so unexpected that leave you in utter disbelief.

In life, you will always encounter situations where you need to rise above adversity. It becomes a confession. A life statement. We have to declare it so that we find our true destiny created for us by God.

I think since 2015, it has been so victorious and vicious all at the same time. It has been overwhelming and overbearing! Just riding down the path of bittersweet. So many half-half's of life. I even said to myself and in the presence of other close friends, "I DON'T WANT TO LIVE ANYMORE!"

But we are not the owner of our days, God is! And He knows us and has numbered our days.

I write this now for all those that suffer with such tremendous loss. For all the deep hurt and deep wounds. People that say... "this is the worst!"

When you come into a complete wreck! A pain beyond recognition! So unexpected, unbearable, unbelievable, uncomprehending, uncompromising... and unyielding!

When does it end? How do you rise above and beyond adversity? As many become gripped with the reality of "no more!"

Death and destruction.
Despair and agony.
I wish this could be lifted off you right now as fast as the sudden blow and sharp sting of pain hits your very life.

What can I say? Anything helpful? Not so much. But here is "something". Here is my attempt. Some little voice and contribution of collective thoughts of compassion and heavy consideration from your powerful pain. As Levi Lusko wrote, "Where there has been impossible pain, God always gives incredible power" in his book "Through The Eyes Of A Lion."

The voice of God whispers to us in these devastating moments of life.
I'm sorry. I'm so sorry that you have to go through this. Not knowing, not perceiving and not ever expecting!

Your plans were completely ruined. Your heart was torn into so many pieces. Your life was shattered. Because it was your heart that was attacked so ferociously, fiercely and so violently. I am so sorry for your pain. I am so sorry for your loss. I am sorry that you have to suffer such severe tragedy when you never even deserved it because you are good.

What Happened?

Life happened. Humanity happened. Death happened. Absence happened. Illness happened. Emptiness happened. The unexpected happened. For us--we lost a general. A backbone to our family. Suddenly. Tragically. Unexplainably.

On April 2nd, we had met the most adverse moment where we needed to RISE as a family. I knew that it would be the worst day that both brothers one in Florida and one in New York were in the same spirit preaching their hearts out. Only one would survive by the end of that day. Only one would hear the news that their life was forever altered. Only one would feel the bottom floor pulled out from them in that moment. Only one would now have to be the leading male role to carry the Mendez family through this storm.

I know others reading this too will know the exact time

they had to fight deep within to rise above their own adversity as well. They had to declare it by their steps.

God knows all things and here is what He declares to us:

I knew that.

You wanted others to know your pain exactly but they did not. If and when they did, nor did it do anything. But to Me it meant everything.

Did you know that?

I saw that you cried so much that you had blood blisters. The vessels popped out your lovely face as it became swollen from the uncontrollable and aggravating tears.

I saw that. You had no sleep, no food and no gym life in you to do a thing.

I saw that. You had no friends around when you needed it the most.

You had no fellowship, no fun and no freedom.

You had nothing to relate. Because nothing was giving you back any life.

I knew that.

That was when I was able to do something when you were down to nothing.

Because you had so much in your life, in your hands and on your mind.

So in order for Me to work effectively in your life yes, you were stripped down to the bone! There I saw the stone. The stone that was created in your heart. From all that pain and sadness. From that moment, I was able to move and begin my deepest and most eloquent work as everything else was being chiseled away.

It hurt. I knew that. And it still hurts you now. But that is because everything that you have belongs to Me first! It is not just yours. It never was. Only the love that I can provide to you can reach you in ways that no human or thing could ever.

I am a jealous God. I want you for Me. No matter what and no matter who is around.

You asked "For how long?"

You asked "How long will I endure this pain?"

I will tell you again until you learn how to live with Me. Until you know to abide in Me for apart from Me, you can do nothing.

I want you to have everything. I want you to bear much fruit not pain because of My great love for you. I can't stand to see you this way. Please know that. Experience ME at work in your life. You will know me in the richest, intimate and powerful way that you have ever known in a lifetime.

Wear this well It is called "Us." Because these moments will be like My own personal love letters straight to you. Already written. Already predestined for your victory. I have purposed you and repurposed you. You will rise again because I am in you. You will make the highest declaration by means of getting up again to fulfill your destiny. And a powerful destiny at that. You will be a great witness. You will be a life testimony.

I knew that then, I know this now…but it is time where I need you to know this and understand this worth. ♥

The Word:

Job 23:10
"But he knows the way that I take; when he has tested me, I will come forth as gold."

John 15:5
"I am the vine; you are the branches. If you remain in me and I in you, you will bear much fruit; apart from me you can do nothing."

Jeremiah 31:3
"The Lord appeared to us in the past, saying: "I have loved you with an everlasting love; I have drawn you with unfailing kindness."

WE RISE!

CHAPTER 1
ANTHONY: OUR GLADIATOR

> "I think ones like him God just decides He's ready to have their friendship in heaven. He just couldn't wait any longer." – Kari Jobe

Dear Antonio Juan Mendez!

This day I mustered up the words that were so difficult to articulate! I will never say goodbye! I will say, I love you my brother all the time! Such a

GIANT in everything!!! Because of you, I'm going to live a little more; because of you, I'm going to laugh a little more because of you, I'm going to love a little more.

I've always seen those three together "live, love and laugh" and I can realize and understand this day that you did that! In your 35 years... you truly lived it 100 fold. Every day you had, you seized it! For none was wasted! It's like you said even in your bad days you made sure you were going to strive to be the "baddest!" And I love that about you. Always pushing to be the best in whatever state you were.

You accomplished in 1/3 of a life span what others could never accomplish over triple that time. Often myself, stood in awe like HOW, WHY.... what is so different? But this week has brought me a TOTAL understanding of that. Because GOD IS GOD and He numbers our days. So now we know in completion that God accelerated you above the rest because He wanted to TAKE YOU TO BE WITH HIM just like Enoch! Because you walked so closely with God and were his loving worshiper!!!

He prophesied over you and your legacy. It came to pass!!! You planted! You went international! You have a beautiful family, home and church!!! You preached like crazy! Taught! Equipped your family, your friends and your church! You helped to save the lives God showed you to and then God knew!!!

He knew He needed to take you.

He knew it was going to be like that.

21 / Anthony: Our Gladiator

So He put you in a deep sleep! It's so unexplainable that we know He took you PRIOR TO THE CRASH! And only your body remained and was damaged... not you!

Not you!!!!

You excelled daily! Your passion blazed across the nations! It is stamped on our hearts! We will never be the same again... not out of sorrow but out of APPRECIATION to the man God made you to be.

Every day you loved your family like crazy!

In your busyness, you made SUBSTANTIAL time for them including them in your authentic, authoritative and audacious world! It was so orchestrated by the Love of God because it was uncommon! Your love for Nelida your beautiful mommy!!!! Your love for Cristina your brave, beautiful and fierce wife! Your love for your amazing children Ezekiel, Isaiah and Ezrabella was evident!!! Your love for Juan was exemplary!!!!! Honorable!!!! He was like your dad and bestest friend in this planet!!! You told him EVERYTHING!!!! Even in a moment's call you filled him in!!!!! Cassy and Sammy you loved them more than life too!!! They were your kids!!! They have your humorous, humble and hunting DNA to ACT without thinking!

And us wow! What can I say? Except that I loved every word that came out of your mouth, the sound of your coughing laughter!!!! We were the greatest siblings on the planet!

I looked up to you! But you looked up to me... WHY??? I will never know that .... So much so, you selected a wife with the same name!!! It was PERFECT! Just like God wanted!

You lived to the fullest ANT!

You laughed the LOUDEST!!!

You loved more than anyone else in this family and that teaches us! You are the true PIONEER of the Mendez and Montalvo legacy!!!! A huge Kingdom General! Our Gladiator!!!! You even carried others when you needed to be carried yourself! I want to do more because of you. And I want to do it right. I have such a clearer understanding of why God gave you "Heaven On Earth" here. It explains so much.

Now I know.... your anointing is here, laughter is here and so many more tasks that you will see come to fruition!

So God sat you down, called you in the midst of this fast paced world and took you to your new glorious home! I love you ANTHONY!!!! So much! I know you knew that and cherished that too. But He loves you more than I could ever or anyone else for the matter because His love is sovereign. I do want to state somewhere in black and white I miss you! I miss our conversations. I miss the huge hugs you gave me that almost hospitalized me from the neck because you were so tall! I miss our opening conversations that always began with a long "YOOOOOOOO" until we couldn't breathe anymore! LOL. I miss us! Our family our friendship and our love for life together because you made the Mendez family feel so legendary in every way. I hope to do that. I hope to be that. I am going to try my best Zearnt...I could always make you laugh! So now I write using my kids impression voice…. "Hey Anthony!"

I promise to pick up where you left and love the ones you loved so dearly! I promise to RISE! You will be so proud of me.

In His Name.

> "With God there is no pain without purpose."
> **Pastor Tony Mendez**

RISE ABOVE ADVERSITY / 24 ◆◆◆

CHAPTER 2
RISE ABOVE ADVERSITY

> "We are beautifully made but tragically broken."
> – Trip Lee

R- Resilient

I- Intentional

S- Salt

E- Emerge

Our days of walking with our head down shall cease.

You must be aware that there is nothing ordinary about you. You are complex, unique and multifaceted.

There are things only you can do the way that you do it. You are important! You matter! You are integral! Without you, there is something missing, something lacking, something broken.

And God is just trying to get us to be the most effective for the Kingdom and that takes WORK.

Many times we rise and fall. We fall and then we rise again! It is a part of life. It teaches us and makes us stronger through God. It teaches us that it is okay to not think we are perfect.

"Even we adults prefer operating out of strength rather than our weakness. But God keeps allowing us to be in situations where our weakness shows. Why? Because only in our weakness can we know His strength." Christine Caine

Unstoppable Devotional January 8

To **rise** is to get up from a lying, sitting, or kneeling posture; assume an upright position; to get up after falling or being thrown down; to be built up or constructed.[1]

So we RISE! We rise above adversity! Every time we thought we would quit, we got up! We had to take our own steps of faith. And as painful as they were or still may be it is exactly where this becomes our declaration to our destiny.

There's purpose!

The acronym I have for **RISE** is also going to be what we declare over our lives which is to come into our destiny. We declare, receive, we do it!

First used is the word **resilient**. I love the description of

---

[1] All definitions taken from dictionary.com

resilient. It means to return back to the original position after being bent, compressed or stretched. It is to recover readily from illness, depression or adversity it is buoyant. A buoy is something that actually floats in the deep waters and never sinks. That is the way that we are when we are IN CHRIST through the deep and dark times of life. In our painful process we become transformed. Trials tell us who we are. This helps us to grow. We never sink. Even when we feel like we are down to nothing…we remain afloat in God. We are able to take on another day, another moment, another task that ultimately leads us to another victory.

We also have to be **intentional** in our walk. As the days get harder we learn how to do things on purpose. There has to be a reason why we do what we do. Why we need to **live on purpose**. Everyone has potential. But potential is perishable, persistence is purposeful. So we have to strive to do things on purpose. We do things consistently. We do it steadfastly, fixed in our purpose and a single direction called progress not perfection.

The bible also speaks to us about being the **salt** of the earth.

"You are the salt of the earth; but if the salt loses its flavor, how shall it be seasoned? It is then good for nothing but to be thrown out and trampled underfoot by men. You are the light of the world. A city that is set on a hill cannot be hidden. Nor do they light a lamp and put it under a basket, but on a lampstand, and it gives light to all who are in the house. Let your light so shine before men, that they may see your good works and glorify your Father in heaven." Matthew 5:13-16

We need to be different. We can't do things the way that everyone else is doing it. We are salt. We are light. Salt has weight...it is heavier than pepper. It is lighter than other ingredients. Once you put even a drop to any form of food using salt the taste changes immediately. When you are in a room, something ought to be different about you. The way you speak shouldn't be the same way others do. The way you respond should be different, positive, effective. We need this salt and light the same way that Daniel and his friends had in the book of Daniel Chapter 1. They were exceptional. Salt makes us exceptional.

Lastly, we will also **emerge**. Because we are resilient, intentional and like salt, we will come forth into full view. We will now be seen. God is not going to allow us to be seen if we are still a mess. But those that conquer and rise in any difficult circumstance, you will certainly stand out as a champion. I know that it is difficult, but you can! You can smile again, laugh again, love again, sing again, dance again and enjoy life again even through adverse times.

The truth of the matter is most people cannot handle adversity.

Most people don't know how to overcome.

Most people live a sick cycle of relapse.

Most people keep going back to bondage.

Most people can't move past pain or hurts.

Most people stay angry.

Most people walk around feeling neglected and bitter.

Most people don't want to let go.

Most people don't know how to get out of their negative thinking.

Most people don't read the Word.

Most people don't know where to go or who to turn to.

Most people don't know how to call on God.

Most people don't know how to live.

Most people don't know how to PRAY!!!!

They keep becoming prey because they don't pray!!!!

Most people don't know how to fight the right way! They don't understand that their weapons are MIGHTY IN GOD for pulling down all these strongholds and for casting away every negative thought and argument that tries to exalt itself against the knowledge of God (2 Corinthians 10 paraphrased).

To cast is to throw! It is to use force! There is work involved in throwing away and off! There is force used to counterattack all those things that try to weigh us down. All those things that try to take us off course and away from our

God-given divine purpose.

We need to learn how to stand up in the face of adversity!

These things happen so we can learn.

Because we are champions.

We are not a victim of our circumstances.

We are the victor.

We are victorious.

We are change agents!

Able to do! Able to make things work!

Coming back from a youth conference in early December of 2017, one of the keynotes Jeff Grenell said, "In hardship learn to worship! Our chaos becomes His canvas!"

This was just another reminder that there is a way! After he lost his wife to cancer he thought life was over. Ministry was depleted! But in that vulnerable situation…. ministry actually BEGAN for him! God uses us greater when we are down to less! So we have to learn how to express our gratitude to God and find LIFE! The life He wants us to live.

Pastor Cristina Mendez of HEIM told the world, "I will still roar! I got more fights in me!!!" This is after losing a husband!

31 / Rise Above Adversity

Pastor Juan Mendez shouted just weeks after losing his brother, "Grow through what you go through!" And continues to uplift the church God gave Him MUI, Yonkers.

Levi Lusko said after his 5 year old daughter past just 5 days before Christmas, "The day I closed her eyes was the day God opened mine!" And he lives every day to preach the gospel!

Now what are you saying?

What are you doing to help change your situation? What are you doing to help broaden your perspective?

All these people with heavy trials are still preaching, still raising kids, still filling the church and they are still living for God! They are impacting nations. So can you.

Get up and stand in the face of your difficulty! Face the adversity! Rise above it! It is not over!!!! God is just beginning His BEST work when you feel like there is absolutely nothing that is going to work!

We had to believe this personally as a family. It was not easy to wait when we got the call that Anthony passed away. He was only 35 years old. Just launching a major movement in the state of Florida through Heaven on Earth Church. Leaving three kids at the age of 10, 4 and 2. It was difficult to wait the hours from 7:30 pm that night rushing all our immediate family to the house to break the news. I will never forget the look on my husbands face. I will never forget telling my daughter and son that their uncle passed away. If only you knew how KNIT this family is. Anthony was the same as their dad! That's how close we all were. He was not only my brother-in-law but a BROTHER! A best friend. A mentor.

We all screamed so much. The vehement cries and agonizing torment of pain that stung our hearts. We held each other for hours. Until we got our tickets to fly the next day very early at 6:00 AM to Florida to meet our grieving family Cristina, his beautiful yet torn wife and his kids. That night was forever. The time was so long. It felt like years to get to Florida from New York. We we're in complete disbelief! How could this be! It's like living a bad nightmare and never waking up.

The hours were dark. My husband and I got no sleep. Just crying through the night. Texting family, sharing our deepest thoughts, prayers and condolences. Still in complete shock from the sudden tragedy. A vicious car accident that immediately took his life as he fell asleep in the car just coming back from dinner after a powerful Sunday Service.

Like who could know that?

They were waiting for him at the house to return as the family took two cars to be at church. Anthony went at 6:00 AM early to lead the church in Morning Prayer. They were on a 40-day prayer journey. It was the 30th day.

But it was also his last day on this earth.

When we met Cristina, his wife in Florida, we came to find

her in front of the house. It was about 11:00 AM and she was held tight no shoes, jeans and a tee shirt just sitting on the concrete. The screams were coming in and out with shocking grief and torment. She yelled continuously and cried tears that shook our soul "I WANT MY HUSBAND!!! GIVE ME MY HUSBAND! I NEED HIM HOME!!!"

It was pure agony for us. Anguish.

Anthony's mother Nelly was there crying on the floor with her sister Mina. I went to hold Cristina and whisper so gently.... "I am here. I'm here with you now." This would be one of many that I would clutch my sister so tight to try my best to calm her soul. Because the cries and screams would just grow louder as we tried to settle the soul of this woman of God. So shattered. So torn. So brutally ravaged by the deepest pain. Every piece of the process was the worst.

From looking at the body next day, collecting his jewelry, wallet to picking out his outfit for the funeral. From visiting the body again for appearance on the funeral day to viewing the remains of the crushed car. Shattered pieces of glass could only demonstrate shattered pieces of her heart as we collected his personal items from the totaled car. My husband had received his last text from him that Sunday as he had a huge smile with his cousin in town. That was the last living photo we saw until we got the photo of him in the crash with no life in him. It was the worst photo to ever receive from a person that knew him. They sent us the image that week truly afraid to send it. It was hard. But one we needed to see as all the pieces still remained unanswered.

Especially the "Why?"

It just happened!

He fell asleep behind the wheel as he was going for a cup of coffee before heading home. That's all. A cup of coffee!

I couldn't stand to see him when we viewed his body. Cold. Life taken. No soul left inside his huge body. He was tall and big. He towered over everyone. But I stood there as I watched his wife cradle his body still and touch all for the very last time as she wept profusely.

His mother looked on in disbelief. Tears unending running down her cheeks. My husband held them back as much as he could. I would only see him cry when I searched for him in the night hours. He stood with a small towel to cover his face in his brother's office crying and praying every night until we left Florida.

This tragedy surely made all look like everything was over for us.

We needed God more than anything at that moment. We needed our family and closest friends to find life still in existence beyond the pain and reality of our loss.

God raise us up. Help us rise above this.

For us all even you. God will make you RISE above it!

CHAPTER 3
RECALIBRATING

"You become dangerous to the enemy when you are fully awake to God."
– Lisa Bevere

I can recall a counselor asking me a question recently over the tragedy of losing my brother-in-law. She asked me, "Have you allowed yourself to grieve?"

Thinking of that now tears still sting my eyes because I

miss him so much. I miss his voice, his laughter, his love, his words, his hugs, his impact, his encouragement and his presence. I miss his very life! Whenever I felt like nothing he would surely make me feel like I was everything.

I miss him. So much. His wife misses him. Who could even understand? My husband will never be the same again. He truly misses him so much. Tells me often. His mom! WOW! That is just a lifetime pain. A lifetime. His kids! The oldest texts him still every night. Misses him so much. He says, "I love you Dad!"

His other son Isaiah would ask, "Why can't I just call Daddy in heaven! He always has his cell phone!!!"

Baby Bella… still waiting for her Daddy at night. She misses him still. It is as if she sees him many times. She says to mom "Daddy!"

Only God.

Only God can fill us now.

It is going to be a year now!

May God do such a work when lives are torn.

The Word of the Lord declares--

Isaiah 41: 15-16

"Behold, I will make you into a new threshing sledge with sharp teeth;

37 / Recalibrating

You shall thresh the mountains and beat them small and make the hills like chaff.

You shall winnow them, the winds shall carry them away and the whirlwind shall scatter them,

You shall rejoice in the Lord and glory in the Holy One of Israel."

You shall thresh the mountains....

The Lord says, you are coming into a season of your life where He has shaped you over the years.

He is about to sharpen you. He is about to make you strategic.

He said to me to tell you that you will begin to function in a more strategic place.

You are going to begin to be more influential in the body of Christ and in the city.

The Lord said to tell you that He is recalibrating you, He is resetting you,

For greater effectiveness!

I heard Deborah, I hear Deborah!

The same mantle upon Deborah, to rally a nation to war, to rally men to war God says I have positioned you in a place that you will rally even men to war.

This was a word given to me on Sunday September 10th, 2017 spoken from Pastor Gideon Mba, Manifold Church (Lagos Nigeria).

I cried so much in that moment. For many times even I for various reasons feel forever pained.

I feel like that turtle too most times putting myself back in the shell for protection and isolation. Then I don't want to do a thing. Emotions take flight.

It is not that I do not want to speak or share but realizing in the interests of many, sometimes I become so intimidated I fall in the place of silence. I then rather not speak so often. I would rather not do a thing. But isn't that how most of us are? We continue to give life to a situation leaning toward negativity. It becomes toxic.

I am leaning towards whatever happened in the past, God used it and has put an expiration date on it. No matter what it was. When it's over it is over. Nothing we can do by going back to change it even if we wanted to. A huge lesson learned, for even in our moments of weakness He intervenes and we all know why. Most importantly, where our place really needs to be.

As for me this process ranges from life incidents to thoughts. Many of our thoughts need to be cancelled out immediately and not shared. The fact that I am walking through a process of ruminating becomes frustrating to me more than anyone else. The one affected by this is me more than anyone else. I need to be well, get well and stay well. I do apologize for ever upsetting others and even myself in moments of madness. I can acknowledge that it is not always our intentions but that it still tends to happen. However one may see it in most cases feelings are always going to present. I wish that was not the case but in that aspect it is! This is exactly where we must push through in our prayer time and in our walk that God has for us.

I had to battle through a lot of thoughts and many other difficult situations. Less of this and less of that. It is not fair to fight this way. It is not fair to me. Most times I feel like less of a woman in those moments. Less wanted. Less influential. Less impactful. Less anything. Always pushed aside by many history repeating itself and finding myself alone most days. But that is my own personal battle. In this state, there are no words to appease any of that.

"I want all of us to feel less alone and more comfortable in our God-sewn skin and a little surer we are a force to be reckoned with in this world."

Holley Gerth Day 1 Fiercehearted, 21 Day Devotional

I know where I stand. I know what it is for me to have to move forward. It is a painful place. But one I must learn to endure. King David experienced his alone times where he had to fight independently.

"And David was greatly distressed; for the people spake of stoning him, because the soul of all the people was grieved, every man for his sons and for his daughters: but David encouraged himself in the Lord his God." 1 Samuel 30:6 (KJV)

In this place when things don't go our way it is rejection. Rejection in any way can certainly be protection. But it still FEELS like rejection. This is a very familiar place that sucks so bad. I remember moments where I would get so dressed up on the outside I did everything to beautify myself. But inside I would be such a mess. I felt like if I put myself well together outside then no one would see clearly what was happening on the inside. So many moments of crying inside where no one can see or hear. These days then became the worst days of my life that press on my mind.

I THOUGHT I looked beautiful...felt that way for a moment. I thought this would help. I thought this would make me drown out what was really happening on the inside of me. But then the reality would hit. No matter how much work I had to put in to be beautiful outwardly, people still went on about their ways and I would still be in that position where I felt so unloved and unimportant. That is the largest dagger to my soul. I don't want to be in that place again.

Life at times can be so disheartening but you know what I know that I am going to find peace in my own version of beauty, in my brokenness (AGAIN), in my pit, and in my own war that was superbly created for me. Rejection is always going to race around me. Mockery. Failure. Disappointments. Unfulfilled tasks. Now I got to learn how to push past all this and really... REALLY be more mindful of that glaring truth. Many will abandon us but never God. Many will not love us but never God. Many will reject us but never God. Many will disappoint us but never God. He is only redirecting us! All these "RE's" I am finding myself in. And I heard screaming in my soul RE-calibrating you… RE-setting you! I'm like, "Wow AGAIN LORD!" I have to seek Him in these moments of violent warfare. Here is the RE it means preposition, in the matter to introduce again and again and again! Until we get it…the part that is continuous is that part that is necessary for us to become the EXPERT!!! So now we have RE-demption! We have reconciliation. We have renewal, restoration and recovery!

He is recalibrating me! Resetting me.

I have to think now that I have been rebuilt for battle!

I will find rest somehow in the battles! And when it is time to rise up then I rise again! I can't stay down. I can't stay silent. I can't stay the victim! I am the victor! I have overcome! These thorns are ways for God to increase and present His strength in me, through me and for me! That will be my place of peace. So when I pray in my madness He will sit with me there too, until I rise again. He is recalibrating me. Again and again. I have to love His persistent effort over my life. I must be important to Him indeed!

They won't rise, until I **rise**!
Villagers in Israel would not fight;
they held back until I, Deborah, **arose**,
until I **arose**, a mother in Israel.
Judges 5:7

RISE ABOVE ADVERSITY / 42 ◆◆◆

CHAPTER 4
OVER AND OVER AGAIN

"I don't know what the thorn was. I don't know, I don't care. Some people say Paul was blind or had a physical infirmity. The bible doesn't clearly tell you what the thorn is because it doesn't really matter, if you are getting hit in the face. A punch is a punch. Attack is attack. Wrong is wrong. Hurt is hurt."
– TD Jakes

"And lest I should be exalted above measure by the abundance of the revelations, a **thorn in the flesh** was given to me, a messenger of Satan to buffet me, lest I be exalted above measure. Concerning this thing I pleaded with the Lord **three times** that it might depart from me. And He said to me, "My grace is sufficient for you, for My strength is made perfect in weakness." Therefore most gladly I will rather boast in my infirmities, that the power of Christ may rest upon me. Therefore I take pleasure in infirmities, in reproaches, in needs, in persecutions, in distresses, for Christ's sake. For when I am weak, then I am strong." 2 Corinthians 12:7-10 New King James Version (NKJV)

So I picked up a new book by Trip Lee called "Rise." It was pretty powerful by the time I got through with it. Finished this one rather fast within the week. Normally what I do when I go into a bookstore is open the book up somewhere in the middle and start reading a few paragraphs! Here is what I found:

"Why do we feel the need to pretend like everything's all right? Because we replace God's glory with our own, and we replace contentment in His acceptance with the approval of other people.

Recently I sat in a physician's office and talked with the doctor about a health issue I've had for a while. After she prescribed some new medications, she asked me a series of questions to make sure I was doing fine otherwise. I appreciated her inquiries, because she was trying to care for me as my doctor. If there had been something wrong, she could have acted immediately. The dumbest thing I could have done is hide my ailment from the very person appointed to help me with it.

Yet we're often tempted to make a similar mistake with our spiritual health. God has given us one another to help fight our sin, but we often hide from each other in shame. That's an understandable response for those who are still exposed and vulnerable to judgment. But our sin has already been covered, so we have no need to hide it. Why hide a bill that has already been paid?"

The point of this message is to remind us, WE ALL HAVE ISSUES STILL!!! But we continue to fuel the lie and pretend like everything is okay all the time. We are afraid to speak, afraid to share and often times mindful to keep things back because it truly seems so redundant.

"You mean to tell me you're STILL struggling with this???"

Well, quite honestly HECK YEAH!!!! I still have to fight! Hello! My sin has been paid for not the process. Then we continue to hide because we can't find a healthy safe "over and over again" place. Like how can I go through this with some "over and over again" folks. That when I explain my "over and over again" not making sense type situation... THEY GET ME!

So here is the big lie folks
"YOU'RE THE ONLY ONE LIKE THIS!"

Everyone has already conquered this the pastors, the leaders, your friends... that amazing and powerful speaker!

YES THEY OBTAINED IT BUT I CAN'T?!?

It is about "Pressing Toward the Goal."

Not that I have already attained, or am already perfected; but I press on, that I may lay hold of that for which Christ Jesus has also laid hold of me. Brethren, I do not count myself to have apprehended; but one thing I do, forgetting those things which are behind and reaching forward to those things which are ahead, I press toward the goal for the prize of the upward call of God in Christ Jesus. Philippians 3:12-14 New King James Version (NKJV)

How do the lustful help those in lust?

How do the stressed relate to those stressed out?

How does the overcome preach about overcoming?

How do the depressed reach the depressed?

How do the anxious help those struggling with anxiety?

Because they have gone through it too or even still go through it that is how.

Here is what I will never forget my mentor, Femi Adun advising me "Only one who has been restored can restore others." Most times I say to myself, "Well have I? Why do I always feel broken though??? Why do I always feel like less in a mess!"

You know why, because I am human! And so are YOU! We are not Jesus! He walked this earth flawless and paid the ultimate price FOR US knowing that we could never accomplish that on our own… so He paid for all the "over and over and over again" type situations!

You are not alone. You have a body of people that can help you but here is how… by being open! By allowing yourself an opportunity to share and allowing others to share with you. By being a trustworthy person. By understanding how to listen and share for the betterment of our process called growth.

47 / Over and Over Again

You cannot heal what you continue to conceal [Rebuilt: Beginning the Ending.)[2]

I mean the enemy does move in to attack us over and over and over again. So what can we do over and over and over again? We can repeatedly share. Repeatedly seek help. Repeatedly go to His word. Repeatedly cry out to Him. Repeatedly pray. We can do all those things until there is a BREAKTHROUGH! Remember the only way to get THROUGH is by the BREAK that goes before it. And in our brokenness we find the most beautiful things. An amazing, unique, gifted, talented, giving, sharing, loving version of who God made you to be!

Now I have to use ALL that I can to think and do positively over and over again. I use the things God gave me and that is a powerful Bible, an amazing family, a thriving church and a body of beautifully gifted sisters that can strive with me.

So my struggles may seem redundant. But so is my God! He is extremely redundant at keeping me all together. About reminding me of His word. About surrounding me with people that are just like me and can relate with me. I am NOT alone. I am in that over and over again place of complete and total victory the same way that you are too.

TD Jakes said in his preaching "Secretly Fighting," how these things always happen to us repeatedly so we learn to take it and keep punching right back. It is a fight every day.

---

[2] First book I Authored, published in September 2016

He said, "Whatever you are going to be doing there's always going to be something punching you. And God sent it. Your sparring partner; to stop you from being too impressed with yourself; to stop you from thinking more highly of yourself then you ought; to teach you that you have to go forward without the conditions being perfect. Some of you have had your life on hold waiting on your conditions to clear up and you're thinking as soon as I get this situated then I'm going to do a work for God but what Paul is teaching is that you don't wait for things to get better, you got to go ahead and do the work WHILE you are getting hit in the face…buffeted."

As Job says "though he slay me, yet I will trust in Him." Job 13:15

CHAPTER 5
EVERY TIME

> This hope keeps you spiritually alive during dark times of adversity.
> – Sarah Young, Jesus Calling

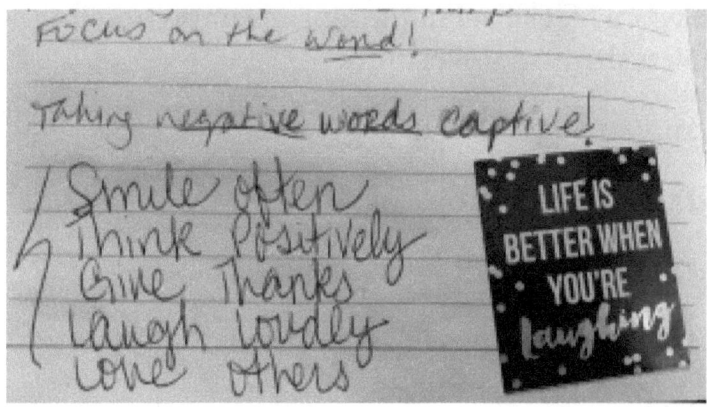

Dear God,

Thank you for EVERYTHING! I even thank You for the pits of life because if it wasn't for them I wouldn't know how to get out. You lead the way EVERY TIME and there is no better place but Your presence. It's in the light of Your love.

I can worship here.

I can be myself here.

I can laugh here.

I can cry here.

I can vent here until every negative word vanishes from my mind.

I can be real with You because You know me.

I can hold myself knowing You are teaching me and guiding me to be a better version of me.

Even when I feel like I'm running on empty You find a way to replenish my soul every time.

I find my strength in You.

I find a way through You.

I find hope, I find faith.

I find the thoughts through Your Word.

I find the peace in the quietness of the days that You give me to sit in silence.

It's uncluttered and empty of the world's busy pace.

Here I find You.

Here I see You.

Here I hear You.

And I listen… I listen intently as You keep reminding me of something so dear and that is Your nearness.

As I go closer to You, You match it!

And even if I didn't, You find me to match it anyway. How thoughtful, how mindful and how great that You are.

You're just trying to get me to that place where I am still in You, settled in You, safe in You, sound in You, secure in You, seasoned in You.

You know it all and got it all.
Every time…
All I need is You Lord.
All I need is all of You.
That works very well.

My soul knows that very well.
Thank you God.
Amen and Amen.

The Lord is my strength and shield.
I trust Him with all my heart.
He helps me and my heart is filled with joy.
Psalm 28:7

RISE ABOVE ADVERSITY / 52 ◆◆◆

CHAPTER 6
BULLET POINTS

> "I wash my thoughts with the truth of the Word of God. I may have to do this several times to get the thought captive." Julie Winter

Be sober [well balanced and self-disciplined], be alert and cautious at all times. That enemy of yours, the devil, prowls around like a roaring lion [fiercely hungry], seeking someone to devour. But resist him, be firm in your faith [against his attack rooted, established, immovable], knowing that the same experiences of suffering are being experienced by your brothers and sisters throughout the world. [You do not suffer alone.] 1 Peter 5:8-9 AMP

Are we really always mindful of where the attacks are meant to hit the hardest?

Mind.

Heart.

These attacks in the mind feel like a strong chemical imbalance. It's too much.

One of my spiritual daughters, Kristen Rabadi sent a word of encouragement to me before I left to Scotland for the second time in 2017.

This trip is going to be good for you. Sometimes you have to get out of your current place changes the scenery. It is helpful. You need that break; need that runaway and to be around your sisters in Christ. This will be rejuvenating for you.

Don't think that you are chemically imbalanced at all. It is not a result to medicine. From a natural standpoint there are things that release those chemicals that make us happy. Dopamine is what will promote happiness like exercise; dark chocolate and more.

I just started a devotional "Detox Your Soul" and the topic is THOUGHTS!

We have these toxic thoughts to be able to overcome toxic thoughts, we need to be able to identify them so that we can then reject them.

Then I looked up the scripture reference 2 Corinthians 10 on **casting down arguments** and every high thing that exalts itself against the knowledge of God, bringing **every thought** into captivity!

God has to help us and fight that fight with us. Because the mind is such a battle.

55 / Bullet Points

Ephesians 6 is another reference on putting on the armor of God.

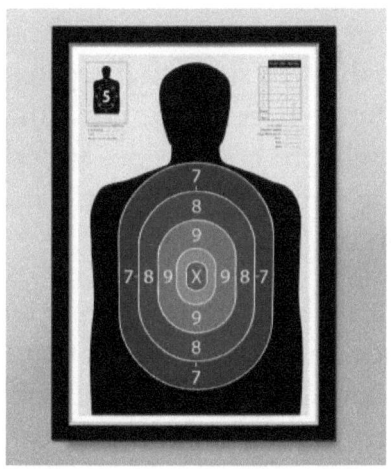

I recently did a lesson with the youth but instead of talking about arrows I talked about bullets to make this more relevant to our modern times. I took the Bullet example drew the outline of the person board from the shooting range places and then explained how vital it is to **not** get injured in your heart or your head.

If your heart gets shot your likeliness of staying alive is close to none.

If your head gets shot (same thing) chances of survival are close to none.

The brain cells don't reproduce and that's why brain injuries are so fatal! People go brain dead and there is no natural way of coming back (same with the spine).

Spiritually it is same thing you get hit in this area or this area your dead.

Spiritually you get hit in this area (heart) or that area (mind), because they are such vital organs you can't afford to be injured there. If cells go, not much of a survival chance which is why the enemy goes after the mind and the heart. This is why protecting the mind and protecting the heart is so important.

Also, it's better for a bullet to go completely through then to get stuck inside and the reason for that is if a bullet gets stuck inside it does something in your body that it is likely to affect the surrounding organs. It is better if the bullet goes straight through and it didn't stay in there.

Using this source: https://health.howstuffworks.com/

A bullet that passes through the body (creating an exit wound) generally will cause less damage than one, which stays in the body, because a bullet that stays in the body transfers all of its kinetic energy (and ensures maximum damage of tissue). This is the aim of most modern ballistic design. Jacketed bullets are designed to fragment after impact, dividing their destructive power. Hollow-point and soft bullets are designed to flatten and spread, creating a wider area for their tracks and increasing the damage caused by shock waves and cavitation.

So with our thoughts it is so much better for it to just go in and right out because if we leave it in there with the impact, it starts to affect the things around it and starts to make our condition worse!

With bullets if you get shot, what makes somebody live? The will to live helps us. For someone that wants to live, a fighter, this plays a big role.

Think about it spiritually. The important thing is that the thoughts go in and out. We don't let it stay in there because that is going to affect our condition more. Just like the bullet. The things go in and they go right out. Don't even entertain it.

Just like the relapse blog[3] on being rebuilt we discover that there is something wrong. We went on this journey and somewhere along the line we messed up. Somewhere along the line something went wrong. Before something didn't work there was a piece that was being rebuilt and then something happened along the way. I have to be rebuilt again and again. That is because there was something that got rebuilt that wasn't supposed to be there. There is something that happened along the way that made this process have to start over.

We can get it right.

Thoughts you have — do you let it sit there? Or do you MAKE it go through?

We understand that our weapons are mighty in God to CAST IT DOWN; it is just a constant thing. We do ask, "Where's my break? Where's my rest?" It gets exhausting. But in God He is SUPER-natural, we don't go dead in any capacity the mind CAN be renewed! OUR BRAINS CAN

---

[3]No More Relapse found on blog site juschrist4.com

BE BROUGHT BACK TO LIFE EVEN AFTER INJURY!!

This is important keeping this (our inspiration) is important. Support keeping that! Prayer keeping that. It's important... they become our ways if we are going to overcome. It makes us stronger.

It's so much harder to fight when you feel like no one is on your side; when you're not being catered to; when they are not showing you love; when no one is surprising you or no one is calling you to see how you are doing. It is so you understand it-wasn't people. There wasn't something that helped you get through it, it was ONLY God!

So now when I'm through it...I had no crutch I had no Band-Aid you had no bandages that helped your healing. Bandages look like your healed but when you take it off it is still not healed. When you take it off-no bandage-raw...nothing covering it.

You did it raw with no medicine, no epidural; you did it raw with no fix.

This is a Spiritual Battle to Fight!

For though we walk in the flesh, we do not war according to the flesh. For the weapons of our warfare are not carnal but mighty in God for pulling down strongholds, casting down arguments and every high thing that exalts itself against the knowledge of God, bringing every thought into captivity to the obedience of Christ, and being ready to punish all disobedience when your obedience is fulfilled.

2 Corinthians 10:3-6

The Whole Armor of God!

Finally, my brethren, be strong in the Lord and in the power of His might. Put on the whole armor of God, that you may be able to stand against the wiles of the devil. For we do not wrestle against flesh and blood, but against principalities, against powers, against the rulers of the darkness of this age, against spiritual hosts of wickedness in the heavenly places. Therefore take up the whole armor of God, that you may be able to withstand in the evil day, and having done all, to stand. Stand therefore, having girded your waist with truth, having put on the breastplate of righteousness, and having shod your feet with the preparation of the gospel of peace; above all, taking the shield of faith with which you will be able to quench all the fiery darts of the wicked one. And take the helmet of salvation, and the sword of the Spirit, which is the word of God; praying always with all prayer and supplication in the Spirit, being watchful to this end with all perseverance and supplication for all the saints. – Ephesians 6:10-18

Note this is the morning information of one of my spiritual daughters--Kristen Rabadi. Great bullet points! Thank you for sharing these words. I won't forget "Bullet in, Bullet out!"

RISE ABOVE ADVERSITY / 60 ◆◆◆

CHAPTER 7
DISCARDING NEGATIVE THOUGHTS

The cost to change is minimal compared to the cost to remain the same ....

I was returning from an amazing trip to the UK, which they would call vacation as a "Holiday"! I would say that this was the best holiday ever! This was the second trip I made out in year 2017 to Scotland but this one was so amazing because it was a getaway from my normal world. I needed the time to reflect, redirect, re-purpose, rejuvenate, re-calibrate, restore, replenish but most importantly renew my mind!

You don't realize how much we clutter our minds as we continue day to day with our busy schedules. It is SO good and so healthy to get away with folks that you don't live with to refresh. There is a time to get away with your family indeed that is a priority time to plan and save as reserved of course. However, time away with friends that you love is truly a time well spent and well deserved. This is bonding with your sisters, brothers or lifelong partners and friends.

They know you, understand you and allow you to take that time to settle your mind. You become a child again. Able to be that authentic loving version that you don't get to put on most days. I have a role as wife, mother, daughter, pastor, business professional and more. It gets so busy for me jumping from role to role. During this vacation it was just me being me…nothing else required. I fell in love with me again. I took the time to de-clutter. I took the time to discard so many negative thoughts that were building up and coming through every act. It was becoming very toxic for me.

I finished reading a book, "Fiercehearted" by Holley Gerth and continued to dive into another good read called, "Renew: Breaking Free From Negative Thinking, Anxiety and Depression" by Julie Winter. This was a hearts cry of mine. Can I be real with that?

63 / Discarding Negative Thoughts

My thoughts and actions were becoming disgusting to ME! Imagine what it was doing to others. I wanted to break free from that and breaking out to another place to reassess, refresh and redo all that was the best decision I could have made. So timely. I think I just reached the brink of a huge breakdown and meltdown that was seeping through. I didn't enjoy being me. I hated to wake up. I hated my thoughts and I couldn't even focus. In a nutshell I fell into another onset of a deep depressed state coupled with anxiety attacks because of my negative thinking!

There's hope!

God led me to pick these books and be obedient to study them. My mind was becoming way too negative for me to function properly. I felt so broken inside so unimportant. I felt less than a person. I felt less of everything. And that is because I kept nurturing and feeding this one big lie that the enemy kept showing me.

"You don't even matter!"

Shaking my head! Well I do matter. I am important. I am loved. I am different. I have beautiful things about me. I am special. I am appreciated. By who? By GOD Himself! And also by me! There are those that love and value me in their life! I am important to God's Kingdom. I have a specific assignment. I have things to do, things to share, things to write, things to teach but how could I do all that with the enemy tearing at my mind, heart and soul ALL DAY LONG???

RENEWAL!

Renew my thinking because it starts within me. In comes the thought Chrizzy flush that crap out! Bad word I'm sorry, but call it what it is. Stinking thinking that needs to be flushed out. Like crap sitting in a bowl down it goes and the smell remains but eventually will disappear into the air and it will smell pure again.

FLUSH IT DOWN AND OUT!

Because that is what the enemy wants to feed us daily when God wants to uplift us daily. It starts in the mind. If you are someone that is being weighed down and bombarded with the thoughts then this is for you too. Don't leave it there. Floating around. Entertaining it...staring at it...rehashing it... keeping it alive... when all it needs to do is flush itself out and be discarded! CAST THOSE THOUGHTS DOWN!!!!

The feelings will then come into alignment with those POSITIVE thoughts. It is time to renew folks renew our mind so that our ways of life become healthy. So that we can have the victory. This "Renew" book reminded me to go to God first to ask Him to reveal the "big" lie so that all the little "reminders" trying to attach itself to the great big lie can be dealt with and discarded timely.

What's the big lie for you? Identify that and use FORCE to cast it down. Make it obey Christ! Make it obey His word! Wash yourself now not with wipes but the water that comes gushing from His Word. That is your life source now and always. To cast is to use force folks! It is to use much effort… to destroy and to tear down. It is work! It is a daily and consistent job! That job belongs to no man but yourself.

More to follow on "Renewing The Mind….." as we keep reading through this necessary material folks. My writer's block has been SEVERED!!!!! "Praise D Lord" as our Grandma Nelly says! Love her. LOL

Let's live again…laugh again…. love again… the right way. Discard every negative thought and begin to love the God that created such a beautiful unique version of YOU! ♥

"Do not be conformed to this world, but be transformed by the renewal of your mind, that by testing you may discern what is the will of God, what is good and acceptable and perfect." Romans 12:2 ESV

"For the weapons of our warfare are not of the flesh but have divine power to destroy strongholds. We destroy arguments and every **lofty opinion** raised against the knowledge of God, and take every thought captive to obey Christ, being ready to punish every disobedience, when your obedience is complete." 2 Corinthians 10:4-6 ESV

RISE ABOVE ADVERSITY / 66 ◆◆◆

CHAPTER 8
WHEN GOOD THINGS ARE NEGATIVE

"It's beautiful!" Beauty can be toxic. Noel Clarke

Driving out of the country part of Scotland, we can once again take in all the beautiful land. So many trees, bushes and green pastures. It's all quite breathtaking. I wish I could stay there. We point to the colorful bushes and say "Look at the many berries on the bushes!" Our guide says, "Oh no you don't want those they are poisonous!"

They certainly don't look poisonous. They look very good. I love berries! I can eat a whole plate of them easily. But no matter how good some things may be, some of it can actually be very harmful for you. There are good things that can be negative we just need to watch for that.

Just like the Word declares:

"All things are lawful for me, but all things are not helpful. All things are lawful for me, but I will not be brought under the power of any." – 1 Corinthians 6:12

So many things are good relationships, food, sports, social media, work…but what about when they have a power over you? What about when they bring you down? Or when the good things take the place of God? Then the good thing becomes negative. Those things are also so hard to let go because they are GOOD! But the negative effect that is occurring because we continue to keep certain things in our lives is not so good for us anymore.

How do we identify those things? Here's a few to help….

Relationships as T.D. Jakes says, "Value is determined by sacrifice." So is this relationship a benefit if there is no sacrifice? Is the person willing to go the mile that you are going for them? Are they willing to lay down some things to accommodate you just the same as you would do for them? Are they willing to change behavior patterns or repeated wrongs? Does that change?

Well there is your answer.

Food

Is this food healthy for you? Are you consuming too much of a good thing? Have you done research to certain types of food that you love that are good? How is your caffeine intake? Your vegetable and protein intake? What if you are loading up on fruits all day? Do you know how much sugar they actually contain? Have you gotten a recent physical?

There is your answer.

Sports

Oh how we love our sports don't we. However, are we damaging relationships that are good to have because we are competitive? Are we becoming too exhausted by them? Are we getting injured by them? Are we taking too much time to contribute to them while neglecting other tasks that are just as important?

There is your answer.

Social Media

This is actually great! We get to keep in contact with family and friends from afar. We get to stay in touch with pictures, videos and more. But are you becoming affected by postings? Are the tags and yearly popup reminders disturbing your soul? Are you becoming sad, angry or frustrated by them? Do you feel excluded? Disliked? Unloved? Is this taking too much of your time by them?

There is your answer.

Work

We all need to make a living. Is your job stressing you out on a daily basis? Are you losing sleep because of it? Are you spending too much time at the work place and finding that you no longer have adequate time to do life?

Well there are some answers. It is not that these things are bad for us. They are good. But when the negative begins to outweigh the good the only thing that you can change at that point is YOU. You can change what you do, how you connect, where you work, the healthy relationships that you can invest in, the food that you can enjoy and the time that you can take for exercise and sports!

Everything has its balance. You just need to learn what is best for you. The key to having a healthy life, is all based on the choices that you make in your daily routine. The things that don't benefit you and begin to pull you down, then take those away. Reduce it. Doesn't mean you have to eliminate the use of good things. Just keep things to a minimum so that you have the best of God's best for you!

You can start today.... When things in your life bring adversity it is time to rise above it and make the things around you positive, by changing the things that can and must.

"All things are lawful for me, but not all things are helpful; all things are lawful for me, but not all things edify."
1 Corinthians 10:23

CHAPTER 9
WHEN NOTHING WORKS

"I have taken you along a path that has highlighted your need for Me, placing you in situations where your strengths were irrelevant and your weaknesses were glaringly evident."
– Sarah Young, Jesus Calling

Do you ever have those moments truly – can I just be honest for a few, when nothing works?

Reading doesn't work;
Writing doesn't work;
Crying doesn't work;
Fasting doesn't work;

All the prayer in the world from you and others over you… still don't work.

That's when you just have to GO THROUGH IT!

I am sure a few of us like me just had to "just go through it…."

Why else would He write down plain for us, WHEN YOU GO....

When you go through deep waters,
I will be with you.
When you go through rivers of difficulty,
 you will not drown.
When you walk through the fire of oppression,
 you will not be burned up;
 the flames will not consume you.
Isaiah 43: 2 NLT

So this clearly tells us there will be moments in life when nothing works. You just have to go through it. It is deep, it is difficult, it is oppression but we won't be consumed by it. Only because God is with us and He cannot be consumed. God is Sovereign. He is sovereign over our situation. He is sovereign over our darkness. He is sovereign over pain and any of our problems.

Just ride it out. Wing it. Do it. Go through. Eventually all will pass and we move onto the next season of life so quickly. What are we going to do reacting to something we cannot change?

It's only for a moment.

Therefore we do not become discouraged [spiritless, disappointed, or afraid]. Though our outer self is [progressively] wasting away, yet our inner self is being [progressively] renewed day by day. For our momentary, light distress [this passing trouble] is producing for us an eternal weight of glory [a fullness] beyond all measure [surpassing all comparisons, a transcendent splendor and an endless blessedness]!

2 Corinthians 4:16-17

This is actually producing for us. This is giving us our own personal powerful purpose in God that is specific to us. Everything will fall into place and everything will eventually make sense. Even if it doesn't now, it will…

Maybe you are still asking why the sudden loss? The job, the person, the finances, the relationships, the credibility, the peace, the joy, the love…. sometimes in one fell swoop we are down to nothing. This is where we have to dig deep beyond our torn emotional realm to tap into the spiritual realm where there is plenty to carry us through.

As I am just coming back from a life changing retreat in the very presence of God, the attacks, blows and punches of life are still coming my way. Every day things will hurt a lot less as I keep pressing in that spiritual realm. God knows all things and made me unique. He loves me beyond measure and beyond anything on this earth. He will uplift me for all the world to see that when nothing else worked, He did just fine. He never left me. Even through my own madness. I love that about God.

When all else has fallen or failed, He is the one that will always remain. So let's just be still. Let's press to keep our soul calm. Sometimes saying nothing works wonders. You didn't get it, well God will give it to you. You weren't thought of, well God is thinking of you always. He will give you the BEST things for your life. He loves to work on a ground that seems useless. This is where pure power is displayed. It is in those broken places.

Did you know that often times the broken places in our lives can be the best places? You may say, "How?"

It gives God a way to show forth His power, His grace, His favor and His strength in us. Yes as you may be shedding uncontrollable tears in this moment but just know that every tear you sow is not to tear you down or weaken you, but it is to build you up and strengthen you…

I think about this family and what we are facing right now and know that God is IN IT! He is the Author and the Finisher. He is the Alpha and the Omega. He is the beginning and the end. And as much as this tries to weigh us down we are still fighting, still smiling, still laughing, still praising God, still ministering and still working through as many raw emotions that try to surface when it looks like nothing is working. What is deeper inside us is bigger than our circumstances.

We have faced hurt repeatedly.

Death repeatedly.

Loss oh a lot more than one can tell. But in and through it all, God has managed to sustain us, help us to rise up and pull out of us all the best. In feeling broken, tattered and torn He has us building a terrific testimony. Our faith will rise above our fear in the most adverse situations.

This will all pass as Nicki Koziarz states in "5 Habits of a Woman who Doesn't Quit," *Victory is often found in the most unfamiliar and uncomfortable places we will find the treasure in the trial.*

We may find ourselves in broken places often we may look at our situations and identify it as idle but it is here that God makes it the BEST places where we encounter His peace, love, power, goodness, faithfulness, gentleness, victory and triumph.

He is working something when it looks like nothing is working. Let's rise up in faith believing in the God of the turnaround!

We welcome this season as we have now been brought quickly to another year and we see His power emerging in us, through us and for us every day!

RISE ABOVE ADVERSITY / 76 ◆◆◆

CHAPTER 10
TIMES LIKE THIS

> "The intensity of the opposition in your life is proof of the power of God's promise in your life."
> – Steven Furtick

Sometimes we may not always be able to articulate what is going through a cluttered mind. You just don't realize how fierce the battle is. It is so violent, so heavy and it floods you until you become completely overwhelmed. You start to sink into the mire.

I thank God that there are so many heroes in the bible that had to have their own personal horror stories on BLAST FOR LIFE! Likeeven past his death we are still speaking of the ups and downs of a King named David. A leader! A guide! A pioneer of faith.

How many times do we recall how flawed Apostle Peter was during his own training days beside the King of all kings. Talk about having the best training ever and still mess up horribly.

Apostle Paul ran churches in every season yet is remembered for his violent temper before and even through his days of Christianity.

They are flawed.

I'm flawed.

Like pretty bad.

I can find myself in a state of distress just like David was before becoming king. To top it all off God sent him 400 more stressed out men to complicate the matter "NOW LEAD THAT WAY!" I'm going to start you up right here! Right in the cave of darkness.

Really???

Even in trying to saturate my mind with the Word of God — the flaws just become so obvious when you are next to the rest. But maybe — just maybe — if we look upon all these written mishaps we will understand just how much they are flawed as you. We are all flawed.

So — God sent His flawless Son to cover all those flaws FOREVER!!!

Every time I want to get better at a thing it looks like I become worse at the thing! I want to rise up above my own tormenting and competing adversity.

I'm going to be a better wife! A better mom! A better friend! A better pastor! I will have a better workout routine...all these betters and it actually becomes worse.

LORD HELP! Just help! Because all of this can be so aggravating to the soul.

What do I do?

Just start again Chris.... start again. You got another opportunity to try it again. No matter how far you think you have fallen, gone off course (mentally, physically or spiritually) just try it again. The greater the loss the greater the victory!

I think many times I don't even know what to do with my complicated self. I often get "leaving you alone". It is so scary. BUT GOD! Thank God that He never tells us "I am leaving you alone." Even in the most silent times, His presence is there to carry us right through the storms of life. Through the storms of our mind. Through any warfare. He will never leave us or forsake us.

So I apologize for being overly complicated. It's not anyone's job to fix that. It is my job to recognize that in His presence I will find the fullness of JOY. I will come up for air and be able to breathe again after my energy is spent laboring away in a bed of anguish.

"Perhaps our eyes need to be washed by our tears once in a while, so that we can see life with a clearer view again."

Alex Tan

Find comfort in His Word, when you go through times like this. He says He will cover you in the wilderness. He will clothe you in the valley. So when I find even my own mind a wilderness and a valley, He is going to cover me and bring me to a place where I will rejoice on every side of the madness that is within.

You crown the year with Your goodness,
And Your paths drip with abundance.
They drop on the pastures of the wilderness,
And the little hills rejoice on every side.
The pastures are clothed with flocks;
The valleys also are covered with grain;
They shout for joy, they also sing.
Psalm 65:11-13

I know these times can be just rough! Between planning, moving and attacks trying to rise up, it certainly becomes a struggle.

As for me, I finally got a quiet moment in what seems to be another challenging yet powerful year. I feel so many mixed emotions and I am trying to drown them out along with a whirlwind of other meshing factors.

Trying to stay positive, productive and functional but speaking frankly, I can get a little tired during these moments. I hate when everything else around me grows so much that it makes me feel like I am shrinking down to nothing.

I don't want to be the "Debbie Downer" but doubt comes so strong to overpower any inkling of mustard seed faith I may have. The small thing should be the driver to get me through. I strive to pass through all the hurdles, curves and distractions of life. But it will get rough.

The times keep ranging to good day… good day…good day… here comes a BIG bad day. And the knot at my throat grows too and the tears of frustration start rolling down. After every victory there appears 10 more valleys!!!

So what am I going to do in a time like this, yes it is further adversity… right now I am going to sit back, shut down and shut up. I'm going to have to settle a bit more inside so I can gather up the strength to use where it will be most necessary. I can't win every battle and every fight but I can still run in the race. Doesn't always promise a win but a finish THAT'S A PROMISE!

It is time to search for that inner peace.

"Therefore, since we are surrounded by so great a cloud of witnesses, let us also lay aside every weight, and sin which clings so closely, and let us run with endurance the race that is set before us, looking to Jesus, the founder and perfecter of our faith, who for the joy that was set before him endured the cross, despising the shame, and is seated at the right hand of the throne of God." Hebrews 12:1-2

Because I started to take such huge leaps of faith, it feels like massive heaps of doubt is trying to overtake me.

What will I do now?

I am going to drown out the doubt.

I am going to drown out the negativity.

I am going to shut my ears to discouraging words.

I am going to close my eyes on gruesome stares.

I am going to drown out the lies with the truth of God's word!

I am going to look away, walk away and back away from all the antagonistic voices that are trying to shout over my victory and progress. I am in a good place. I am better. I can do more. I can obtain it. I choose to believe GOD and not the faces or doubting voices!

Then when the victory comes again this time I will have escaped from the depths of these valleys and moved on to an even place. A God place. All because I know it was the Spirit of God prompting me to take the huge steps of faith!

Watch it work Christina! Watch God work!!!!!

Better days are ahead.

It's time to let go so God can do the rest. Another huge leap of faith! Let's go!

CHAPTER 11
HIS MIGHT AGAINST OUR MIGHT

"A fierce hearted woman... makes gentle the new strong, small the new BIG, ordinary the new extraordinary." Holley Gerth, Fierce Hearted

I used to feel like my own mighty warrior when I passed through certain battles. Through much pain, scars, tears and rebuilds I always found a path for me. Any battle we face that was worth such effort there is no way to come out without a scar. For even the greatest warriors

have wounds. There is EVIDENCE of a fight there is evidence that they had to put MIGHT into the FIGHT! But there is nothing like God's might against our might.

We have to come to realize that the majority of our lives will be in a mode of battle, hardships and struggle. This is part of our growth. This is part of our destiny. There is purpose, even in this.

The bible instructs us that we have to put on the armor of God. The detail of how is clearly listed all throughout Ephesians 6. However, there is this verse that stands out which reads in the New King James Version, "Finally, my brethren, be strong in the Lord and in the power of His might." So I often repeat this to myself when I face opposition of any sort:

"Be strong in the Lord and in the power of His might."

"Be strong in the Lord and in the power of His might."

"Be strong in the Lord and in the power of His might."

I repeat and I repeat. Yet come to the acknowledgement that the enemy is strategic in his ways. Even if it is in one direction in that one direction there are different things you will have to pass through. Am I strong? Am I weak? Can I call it what it is besides pure HUMANITY? We are NOT God! Being like something isn't exactly IT! God is sovereign and sits upon the throne. We are here on this earth fighting an ongoing war day and night.

85 / His Might Against Our Might

By myself I ain't a thing! I AM WEAK! I HAVE MANY FLAWS! I AM IMPERFECT! I MAKE SO MANY MISTAKES. I think I am strong sometimes but then I smack right into my humanity that pushes me to seek further in my spirituality! I am strong ONLY in HIS MIGHT! Because MY MIGHT is not as strong. Because His Might is all powerful...

I might fall. I might mess up. I might not make the best decisions. I might not be the most reliable source. I might lose control. I might go off in some tangent that takes me back! I might do a whole lot of things but one thing I do know is this Word that He gave us. HIS MIGHT IS GREATER! And as long as I keep my eyes ON HIM, look to Him and seek HIM like never before I will find HIS MIGHT working far more exceedingly than my "might" could ever do!

In conclusion, be strong in the Lord [draw your strength from Him and be empowered through your union with Him] and in the power of His [boundless] might. Ephesians 6:10 AMP

How do we really become empowered? We draw strength FROM HIM and not from any other source. Our union must get stronger. More stable! More ABLE! I know that in Him all the mights that I have get cancelled out with the one MIGHT that took Jesus to the Cross to pay the price FOREVER! It is finished! So I love the photo I have from Father's day. It took a lot for me to get there. A lot of suffering, tears, agony and pain but one thing I found was a smile. I found my source of strength IN GOD! I can't allow any one to take that from me ever again not now not ever. I keep coming back to HIM! I need HIS MIGHT over mine EVERY DAY!

"No temptation has overtaken you except such as is common to man; but God is faithful, who will not allow you to be tempted beyond what you are able, but with the temptation will also make the way of escape, that you may be able to bear it." 1 Corinthians 10:13

"The intensity of the opposition in your life is proof of the power of God's promise in your life." Steven Furtick

Just as I requote this saying from Steven Furtick [Elevation Church] it speaks volumes on how we are able to bear and soar through the fierce battles of life....

We are going to win the war! We are going to rise up. Because the promises of God will be fulfilled! Make it your declaration! Trust that. Trust His Mighty power always working on your behalf.

CHAPTER 12
THE WALK

"It's time for you to make your own footprints."
Cristina Mendez, Lionheart Global Ministry

A certain walk,

A certain smile,

A certain peace,

RISE ABOVE ADVERSITY / 88 ◆◆◆

A certain joy,

She'll stand by her King,

JusChrist first & foremost.

Then by the one on earth?

Pave the way through prayers,

Press through work,

Portion what she can,

Bravery becomes her,

Pressure encourages her,

Humility is her familiarity,

Always a game changer,

Breaking through any barriers.

Unlike the pretty,

Nothing like the beautiful,

The only bold she has

Is allotted by the one who called her… the Queens Walk.

She will have her own footprints in this life and the next.

Eternity is at the door.

What better kind of walk one could find as royalty.

You have your own walk to do. As a king or a queen.

I refer to Queen Esther who was handpicked and positioned in the palace for a great purpose when adversity was going to rise. In this small book in the Old Testament a huge victory comes out of it. Because of Queen Esther's courageous act, a whole nation was saved. Seeing her God given opportunity, she seized it. Her life made a significant difference.

In adversity you have to seize the opportunity.

In your position of royalty and importance, what will you do with it?

If you are unfamiliar with this book in the Bible, it is about Esther being selected as a new Queen to replace Queen Vashti that failed to serve the king by appearing at his request. Because of her disobedience she was dethroned and never again seen again. Because of Esther's obedience, not only her but an entire legacy is still thriving from her brave act to stand in the gap.

Esther just needed to respond.

She needed to pray and stand in a place of intercession. The Jewish people were faced with being annihilated because of an evil man name Haman. With a hatred for a man named Mordecai he wished to destroy his entire race. Until Esther was notified of this terrible crime that would come about her relative Mordecai who encouraged her to help by appealing to the King, her husband Xerxes.

"For if you remain silent at this time, relief and deliverance for the Jews will arise from another place, but you and your father's family will perish. And who knows but that you have come to your royal position for such a time as this?" Esther 4:14

She harkened.

What do you do in the face of adversity?

Do you stay silent?

Do you remain idle?

Do you run or hide?

Do you isolate yourself from others?

Why do we keep running from adversity when God is using it to propel us to a higher position and into a great place of victory?

This is the moment to prove your royal position in the Kingdom of Heaven!

This is the time to shine.

This is the time to share.

This is the time to speak.

This is the time for you to intervene in some way to make a difference during an adverse time.

Here comes her declaration:

"Go, gather all the Jews who are in Susa, and fast for me. Do not eat or drink for three days, night or day. I and my attendants will fast as you do. When this is done, I will go to the king, even though it is against the law. And if I perish, I perish." Esther 4:16

She didn't even miss a beat. In verse 14 she had a call to respond. By verse 16 she made a declaration. She seized her opportunity.

What you do in private, God will reward you openly.

Isolating isn't going to get you far.

Interceding in the place of adversity is going to give you AND others the greatest victory ever. So make your declaration today.

Rise above the most adverse moments of your life quickly!

Respond. Get up. Fight with faith! Fight with prayer. You may be in a waiting period sometimes but God is working in every moment to perfect the greatest testimony for you and your household just like He did for Esther.

I know it hurts. I know it is scary and many times so painful. But do it. Trust God and your ability to do more than ever before.

We do more with less. God gives more grace during absence and loss. He gives you more in the midst of mess and chaos. It just becomes His canvas to paint a clear new picture for you. Your divine story of triumph is in that canvas of chaos.

Trust in Him.

Mordecai had done an act that was written in the book of the chronicles. He had exposed two of the king's officers that were plotting to assassinate him. This went unrewarded but recorded.

When you feel like you are doing something great and see no reward just know that God has it recorded!

God saves your reward for the right time!

That is why you can experience delay. It is necessary during a precise time so that it can change the course of adversity in your situation.

You planted! You gave! You sowed!

"You will always harvest what you plant." Galatians 6:7

So in that perfect time during your imperfect walk — God makes it perfect with His plan. Follow through with it because He is doing something glorious during the hard days.

Don't give up now. It is not time to throw in the towel. There is a walk that is so destined for you to travel upon. God has made you just for this purpose.

Man of God rise up! Woman of God rise up!

We are kings and queens in this walk with special purpose.

I know I am discovering mine.

Proverbs 31:10-31 (Recovery Translation)

Who can find a worthy woman? For her price is far above jewels.

The heart of her husband trusts in her, And he will have no lack of gain.

She does him good and not evil All the days of her life.

She seeks wool and flax, And delights to work with her hands.

She is like the merchant ships; She brings her food from afar.

She rises also while it is still night And gives food to her household, And their task to her serving girls.

She considers a field and buys it; With the fruit of her hands she plants a vineyard.

She girds her loins with strength And makes strong her arms.

She samples her merchandise to be sure it is good; Her lamp does not go out by night.

She lays her hands to the distaff, And her hands hold on to the spindle.

She stretches out her hand to the afflicted, And she reaches out her hands to the needy.

She does not fear for her household when it snows, For all her household are clothed with scarlet.

She makes coverings for herself; Her clothing is fine linen and purple.

Her husband is known in the gates, When he sits among the elders of the land.

She makes linen garments and sells them And delivers girdles to the merchant.

Strength and dignity are her clothing, And she happily looks forward to the time to come.

She opens her mouth with wisdom, And the law of kindness is on her tongue.

She watches closely over the ways of her household And does not eat the bread of idleness.

Her children rise up and call her blessed; Her husband also, and he praises her, saying:

Many daughters have done worthily, But you surpass them all.

Grace is deceitful, and beauty is vain; But a woman who fears Jehovah, she will be praised.

Give her of the fruit of her hands, And let her works praise her in the gates.

London 2017

RISE ABOVE ADVERSITY / 96 ◆◆◆

CHAPTER 13
BE GRATEFUL, THANKFUL

> "Once you have become grateful for a problem, it loses its power to drag you down."
> ~Young, Sarah. Jesus Calling

I can't believe how fast we got to the holiday week! Already Thanksgiving. Unbelievable! So many things to be grateful and thankful for. However, in a mind where rumination exists this could be a time of turmoil as the holidays approach. What can we do to counterattack that mindset? We can begin by working diligently to flush out those thoughts and focus on the positive. There is always something to be grateful and thankful for. Even in the lack.

As Apostle Paul wrote:

"Not that I speak in regard to need, for I have learned in whatever state I am, to be content: I know how to be abased, and I know how to abound. Everywhere and in all things I have learned both to be full and to be hungry, both to abound and to suffer need." Philippians 4:11-12

No matter what season we go through we learn how to be content. This is a state of inner peaceful happiness. Instead of thinking so much on the things that we do not have or have been negative, we have to think of what we have left and what is positive. There's life that continues for us and we need to find purpose in that. We can live again, laugh again and love again.

What are we grateful for? What are the things that we can appreciate in our life? There are family, friends and fellowship. There are people that still love us tremendously. There are friends that need your words, your hugs and your time. There are people that we can fellowship with and share encouraging words through times like this. We just have to come out of a state of inactivity to where we are actively seeking the good.

We have to nourish our mind. Not the pain, not the past and not with the things we can do nothing about. We are grateful to have had wonderful memories. We appreciate them. Now we also have the capacity to make new ones.

There is also a big world for us to travel upon. The many places our eyes have not seen to remind us of all the beautiful things that exist. Places to visit, coffee shops to sit in and landmarks to view. This is all for us. We just need to invest the time in travel because there is such a value in viewing new things.

What are we thankful for? What are we pleased and relieved about? I am pleased and relieved that I got through MANY difficult obstacles in life. Which leads me to believe that no matter which ones come my way, there is going to always be a way out. Look at how far I have come. Look at how far YOU have come. We are not the same people, we are stronger! We become a better version of us.

We learn how to move away from rumination, which is the process of deep thought. It is where we encourage negative thinking. We feed it. We keep it alive. We care for it and continue to give it life rather then let it die out.

"If you start looking for good news, you will find it everywhere."

Renew: Breaking Free from Negative Thinking, Anxiety & Depression Julie Winter

So let's start seeking the good. We find that in His word and we find that by changing our thoughts to reflect heavily and purposefully on what we are grateful and thankful for this holiday season. Some people don't even have a warm plate of food, but we do and we can help someone get theirs. They will be grateful and thankful for YOU!

We use these times to be fruitful and helpful.

I had to develop a habit of reflecting on all the things that I have good going on. I have to write it down, meditate upon it, repeat and declare it loudly so that it brings a change to my mindset and situation. Instead of being helpless and hopeless I have to immediately pull something that I am thankful for. There is always going to be something.

We always lean to think some of the worse things when

adversity rises up. "Oh here we go again. This always happens to me. I am never going to get through this."

But what if you do?

What if God is using this to take you to the other side of life?

What if God is trying to strip you from the former things to give you the very thing you have been praying about?

Embrace the newness of the life that God wants you to live. Everyday is not a loss. Everyday is something new and it can be something great depending on how you see things. Don't allow these opportunities to go wasted when His promise will always remain for you to have the greatest victory!

"Adversity brings the opportunity to introduce us to ourselves in a whole new way." Nicki Koziarz

Happy Thanksgiving to all.
"Remember not to eat too much."
– For Jessica Montes De Oca

CHAPTER 14
40 DAYS LEFT

"God has called me to start a 40 day prayer revival on Facebook live at 5 am."
Many Thanks to Pastor Edward Ramirez from Harvest Outreach Ministry in New Jersey for such a revelation to close out the year of 2017!

THROUGH PRAYER!

"I have come that they may have LIFE and have it to the FULL." John 10:10

My prayer for the day, I am going to write this one down.

My prayer for the journey is now going documented for all the world to read.

Dear God, THANK YOU, for my life, my love, my family and friends. Thank you for keeping me in the midst of a very difficult year. You held it down! You managed to still do so much with me and for others. I saw smiles in the midst of massive tears. I heard laughter in the midst of agonizing pain. Thank you because none of us lost our minds in the madness but we found miracles in it. We saw your hand literally over the face of our family embracing us in the chaos. You were there just as the Word declares...

> "Even there Your hand shall lead me,
> and Your right hand shall hold me."
> Psalm 139:10

You're just amazing God because we still have life when we faced death.

We saw light in the midst of darkness.

We see a way in the midst of the deepest valleys.

Your power and glory are there!

So apart from the gratitude here is the simple request that I bring to you in prayer. May You continue to shower healing and great health over the Mendez family, Arvelo family, Ramirez family, Cruz family, Rivera family and the many more families that I am connected to both in the natural and in the Kingdom! We love you and trust you. This is our year for greatness! Why? Because You were there through the most daunting experiences and You are still here now. May the family LIVE, LAUGH AND LOVE well. Let the smiles be radiant and thankful hearts rejoice in this holiday season. Make it happen because You will always be the God of the impossible. Amen and Amen.

This is our time to emerge!

I record this prayer and so many others because through

this online prayer chain it triggered us to have our own for our church. We started 2018 with an online prayer room for members to tap in as we lead opening our day with prayer and intercession. London taps in.

Florida taps in.

Atlanta taps in.

New York taps in.

We tap in to the very presence of God.

Prayer is always going to be key for us. But even more so it can be effective if we do it daily, consistently and as a body. It is not easy but it is possible. Sometimes we go on about our day and get so busy and then we forget about God. We forget to give Him our first fruits of the day. He just wants to spend time with us. Whether it is 40 days left, 40 months, 40 years and so on. This life belongs to Him. We share it with Him.

"Listen to my words, Lord, consider my lament. Hear my cry for Help, my King and my God, for to you I will pray. In the morning, Lord, you hear my voice; in the morning I lay my requests before you and wait patiently." Psalm 5:1-3

This is the lifestyle that He desires for us to have in all of our days. A prayerful lifestyle. When we do this individually and corporately it honors His name which is above every name. It magnifies Him. It exalts Him. So everything that seems small and insignificant now is given in the hands of God through prayer as we magnify His name.

We may think that this is something that we should not do but what we and can do is use it as a positive platform to connect in a prayerful way.

We use media to share food — share jokes — share verses — share selfies and group shots. We share just about anything on all these social platforms. Why not use it to connect together in corporate prayer???

Good idea right!

It works! It is reviving the hearts of people that were not disciplined. Now they are becoming disciplined to wake and log on.

We pray together.

We cry together.

We laugh together.

We petition together.

We touch the heart of God together.

There are so many tools that we are overlooking that could help us strengthen in areas where we were once weak.

We use it to share broadcasts of our services now. We use it to teach, train and disciple. Now we use it to pray together! What a concept. An eye-opening concept for us to grow stronger together in prayer.

There are also other avenues that can be used to join together. There are free conference call lines that you can share with your group or ministry leaders. People can dial in and pray together as well. Then you also schedule your times to meet together in a home or in the church where you can pray together too.

For us at MUI Church our days are Wednesday morning and Friday nights. We use the facility weekly to pray. My husband and I started to pray ever Friday back in 2000 with a couple of our Christian friends. We just kept at it ever since. So for 18 years now our Friday nights are completely sold out to corporate prayer.

Prayer meetings are one of the hardest to sustain. If we were to schedule cook outspicnics and parties those would typically pack out in attendance. But for prayer it is far and few.

Until we become consistent we will not see the results of anything. We see the results. This truly has been a tool to sustain us personally, professionally, financially, within ministry and for our families too.

Prayer is the glue that holds our hearts together through every season of life.

So when you don't know what to do – try prayer. Individually and corporately. Try harder. Be more fervent and intentional about prayer. Build your prayer muscle.

Grow stronger in these pressing days by lifting your voice to the heavens!

God is with you and waiting for you to do just that. Every day left on this earth should be spent in prayer. It is just that important.

CHAPTER 15
CONDITION THE MIND FOR GREATNESS

> It is not enough to have a good idea; You have to execute! – T.D. Jakes

Let us draw near to God with a sincere heart and with the full assurance that faith brings. Hebrews 10:22

Dear Lord, consecrate me for this next season.

Keep changing my mind.

Keep changing my thoughts.

Keep changing my heart.

Keep changing my ways!

Let the last of this year be in COMPLETE JOY for me! Even through the patchy days & cold seasons. May I rejoice DAILY!

I'd say, I never want to cry again.

Then there are tears.

Tears to remind me that I am just human and that You are supernatural.

May I put on love-joy-peace and also meditate in Your Word so there is continuous CHANGE!

Flush my mind with the Word of God – the Word that breaks the chains of darkness.

The Word that breaks the chains of doubt.

The Word that breaks the chains of discouragement.

The Word that breaks the chains of depression, anxiety and any ill thing!

Your Word gives me LIFE!!!

Break the chains that try to shackle my mind.

Break the chains Lord – that every thought is taken captive.

Keep renewing, restoring and rebuilding my mind.

RECALIBRATING

Because it is a constant war. Let the noise of my thoughts settle. If it's not going to bless me now, let me let those things go!

Quickly flush them out of me because those words seal in my heart. I will keep praying and fasting about this! Lord let my mind grow with rich and positive thoughts. Condition my mind for greatness. Leave a positive message branded in my mind Lord.

Words of LIFE, in the name of Jesus.

I need You God! I need You in my thought life.

Because I can't think any other way.

Keep changing my mind.

Dear God, that is my prayer.

Amen

Many people are quick to say, "They didn't do for me." But what did you do for them? Your absence should always be felt.

What kind of contributor are you or are you just looking to receive?

This is something that I ask myself now. Am I a

contributor? Can I do this in a better and greater way?

God is the ultimate distributor so we can become contributors. I have a purpose here on this earth. I have to contribute to the big pie of life. If I condition my mind for this greatness then greatness it shall be.

The Mouth of the Prophet declared,

September 17, 2017 at 12:44 am

Not only will you declare my counter with my mouth but I will cause you to understand ancient wisdom.

I will cause you to understand my mind.

For the scripture says "let this mind that is in Christ be in you."

There are people that have the word of the Lord, but the Lord says not only will you have my word but you will understand my mind.

Because through this I will give you the insight into the deep things of God.

Not only will I give you the insight to the things of God, I will cause your mind to understand this ancient wisdom and be able to interpret them into systems and structures and strategies.

He said I will once again touch your mind like I did with Peter and I will cause you to possess wisdom beyond your age not only spiritual wisdom but I will give you organizational wisdom like never before for the Lord says that you are a builder. And this day I will pour upon you that which it takes to build and it is my wisdom.

For the scripture says "through wisdom is a house built"

Not only will I give you the wisdom to build my kingdom but I will also give you wisdom like never before to build your children.

For the things which they have right now requires the wisdom that I am about to put in you.

He said you will not need to struggle about this but this will be clear that they will need your wisdom.

Because you stand today in an office where my wisdom will justify my call upon your life.

You stand in an office today that my wisdom will justify that I have found you afresh.

He said my wisdom will justify this call upon you today that I have sent you for such a time as this to preserve and to rescue.

I see buildings that are dehabitated and these buildings not necessarily are physical buildings but the Lord says these are ideas, these are ministry codes here.

These are people.

But the Lord says I will give you such wisdom to preserve this people from decadent and from degradation.

For you are a preserver of destiny through this wisdom that I am pouring upon you today.

You are my mind, says the Spirit of the Lord

In the book of Proverbs chapter 8, Wisdom spoke up and said "I wisdom was present in the beginning of foundation and of creation" and the Lord says today the same wisdom that was present at the foundation of the earth that wisdom is poured upon you. Because the bible says it is the same spirit.

Isaiah tells us in Isaiah 11, the Spirit of the Lord is the Spirit of wisdom.

May the prayers of the Almighty God come upon you tonight.

May the prayers of the wisdom of the Messiah.

The bible says for Christ is the wisdom and the power of God.

You have known my power Christina says the Lord.

You have tasted my power Christina says the Lord.

My power has worked in evidence in your journey so far says the Lord but now you are about to come into a dimension of my wisdom.

For He will open your mouth now even within your brothers and your sisters but you will open your mouth even before people that do not know me and from that they will come to know me.

I impart to you today daughter of Zion

The gift of wisdom

The spirit of wisdom

Is being stirred up in your soul tonight

Is being stirred up in your soul today

Scripture says, "A wise women will build her home."

Christina the Lord says, I am raising you up.

Also comes with humility the power to build in your home.

The Lord says I will give you the strategy

He said do not be afraid, Christina.

For the days that are very close before you.

People will judge you, they will say after all she is just pastors wife.

After all she is just a lady.

But hear me clearly says the Spirit of the Lord.

When I chose Juan I chose you.

When I anointed Juan I anointed you.

When I called him I called you.

When I blessed him I blessed you.

When I sent him I sent you.

Never you take the back.

Love your husband.

Honor your husband.

Fight for your husband.

Correct your husband,

In love.

Because I will show you things.

Because it will be a debt for me.

And I will give you the details so that it doesn't become cumbersome to him.

Then when God shows you these things he said tell her, so that with humility of heart you will interpret these things before your husband.

And he will love you and he will bless you.

And he will exalt you before all men.

Because you have honored and you have served Him, says the spirit of the Lord.

Christina, listen to me. The Lord says you have consecrated your finances for my sake. You have showed that your body of my servant. He said, when I sacrificed him I also placed a demand on your finances. Such that you say such times secretly that there are things that I would have loved to do but this responsibility will not allow me to do. But the Lord says, the time has come that you will not even need your salary.

Because the Lord said, I will bless you.

And this blessing will be expressed through men coming to be a blessing to you.

Listen to me Christina, you are not just an employee.

For the days will come that the Lord said you will finally realize that you are an employer of labor. Which was that I have given you the gift of detail. And it will be your strength to help other people. – Prophet and Apostle Femi Adun

I will rise.

I am built and conditioned for greatness says my God.

RISE ABOVE ADVERSITY / 116 ◆◆◆

CHAPTER 16
ATMOSPHERE CHANGER

> Patterns when addressed as if they were only a problem to be solved, remain. Sometimes even addressing the pattern wont change things. That's when a consequence is needed to break the pattern.
> – Nicki Koziarz

So here's what I want you to do, God helping you: Take your everyday, ordinary life, your sleeping, eating, going-to-work, and walking-around life and place it before God as an offering. Embracing what God does for you is the best thing you can do for Him. Don't become so well-adjusted to your culture that you fit into it without even thinking. Instead, fix your attention on God. You'll be changed from the inside out. Readily recognize what He wants from you, and quickly respond to it. Unlike the culture around you, always dragging you down to its level of immaturity, God brings the best out of you, develops well-formed maturity in you. – Romans 12:1-2 MSG

Another day came after work, I left and went straight to Target with a *target* in mind. I want change. Change in my mind, change in my diet, change in my scenery and change in my routine. I really do. As tired as I was I went to get things I had in mind that could help.

I came in today refreshed and positive. I want Christmas here! So here is how my day began:

I woke at 5 am for the 40 day prayer rally with Pastor Edward Ramirez.

I finished with my own personal prayer after the online version ceased.

I got dressed for workout at my own personal gym that I am building in the basement.

I drank my water got showered & ready with new Enagic products.

I got dressed for work and made it a skirt day with some make up.

I jotted down my workout routine in my motivation journal as a tracker.

I made myself my Vega-One protein shake & gathered my food for the day.

I left the house with my coffee and belongings got to work with all the decorations.

As I walked down the corridor with all the decorations in the box my boss smiled and said "Wow, what is all this!?" I said, "I am bringing Christmas here!" She responded, "I just love you for that!"

I decorated the office and soon after the colleagues joined in the holiday fun. I handed out some stockings and we continued to decorate. Everybody's mood was quickly changing and super joyful. All smiles on their faces. We needed some holiday cheer here.

Just as the Word says "Take your everyday and bring it before God as an offering!" When we take a positive approach and change our atmosphere, we are bringing God a GREAT offering. Spreading love and holiday cheer can be every day! Not just in December. Consistency is key. A set mind is key. A smile is key. I need to be more proactive and intentional about changing my environment on the regular. I am happy that I got a lot done so far today.

The rest of the day is set for me as I will continue to listen to positive and uplifting music. I will think on good things [Philippians 4]. I will read throughout the day as is my norm and I will press for productivity. The more effort I put in;

the more results I will see because I decided to change my atmosphere.

I am ready to do it again tomorrow. ♥

I am an atmosphere changer! So are you!

I am tired of routine. Tired of the blah days. I have become so tired of all this time going wasted and not getting enough things done to reach closer to my goal.

The game changer!

ME!

My mind my thoughts my initiative.

Who else is going to take those much needed steps for me.

This is only answered prayer. To see some really good work get settled and done. We need to do better and quit being so complacent.

You know the more I think about this the more I think the one thing I'm quitting at is to do better. I feel like I'm quitting at the potential that I know I have in me is built for more.

Does that make sense???

Why do I feel like I keep resulting to settle?

I settled with this weight!

I settled with this job!

I settled with the place where I'm at in ministry!

I'm settling in life for what everyone else wants me to do first and never consider my own needs!

Like aren't we important too? I know we have this "die to self" emphasis as Christians and I do that... but when will I die to complacency? What about die to settle? What about die to the mundane ways of life? Refuse to sink? Refuse to living with all these insecurities and doubts when I have potential??

> "What a shame it would be for the enemy to believe more about our potential than we do."
>
> Holley Gerth, Fierce hearted 21 Day Devotional

I don't want to keep doubting myself. This feels awful! I know there is more and I know if I am continuously grieving over my situation when I know that I have an option to change it! I can contribute to change the environment and situation that I am in.

Why am I settling???

I'm not a quitter! But there's one thing I want to quit.... COMPLACENCY! There is so much more! If it can happen for others surely it can happen for me too. I'm going to be a little more intentional about moving forward in faith to do BETTER! To enjoy my days. To enjoy the work that I do daily. To enjoy my health. To enjoy the relationships that I have around me. There is so much more!

This is definitely on my prayer list! Maybe yours too?

This can only be answered prayer. To see some really good work get settled and done.

As Bishop Noel Jones preached, "There is something that is going to happen that will negate what you are dealing with right now!"

There's more! There's HOPE! Apart from that, I have to quit at what keeps me complacent!

The bible declares:

"The pain that you've been feeling, can't compare to the joy that's coming." Romans 8:18.

"Rejoice in hope, be patient in tribulation, be constant in prayer." Romans 12:12 ESV

Dear Lord,

Help us break past this spirit of sluggishness and disbelief! Let us QUIT COMPLACENCY immediately and make aggressive steps at better days!

As you desire for us, let there be a huge shift and promotion in business and workplace. Creative ideas coming to fruition.

Entrepreneurship and ownership.

Let ministry be birthed in the city of Yonkers and in New York. Let ministry be birthed in your city. We declare it.

Let us emerge. Let us be exposed. Take us to increase and elevation. Take us to the gate of our destiny. Take us to the gate of our miracle. I know that anytime I want I can cause a prompt. I can get your attention with my faith. By making a change and taking aggressive steps to see ourselves doing more and doing better.

Help us to reach and press beyond the limitations of SELF and our own way of doing things. Help us to break routine, habits and patterns that are not allowing us to grow and go where we need to. Your design for us has always been for more. It is on the tablet of Your heart which is Your Living Word. These inner frustrations and turmoils that are rising up within are only because we are sticking within our own limitations when we know that there is more. We know that we can be more and do more. Help us to reach beyond the limits…because on our own we are going to remain the same. WE WANT OUT!!!!

As Your Word declares:

"Enlarge the place of your tent, stretch your tent curtains wide, do not hold back; lengthen your cords, strengthen your stakes."

Isaiah 54:2

Amen and Amen!

"Never be afraid to try something NEW because life gets boring when you stay within the limits of what you already knew."
@Facts Twitter

RISE ABOVE ADVERSITY / 124 ◆◆◆

CHAPTER 17
BECAUSE OF OUR CHAINS

> "As a result, it has become clear throughout the whole palace guard and to everyone else that I am in chains for Christ. And because of my chains, most of the brothers and sisters have become confident in the Lord and dare all the more to proclaim the gospel without fear." Philippians 1:13-14

Because of our chains; Because of our despair, Because of our pain; Because of our struggle; Because of our mess it actually inspires others when we are able to go through those things triumphantly. People can say "Wow! They conquered that!"

They weren't hidden chains that Paul had. Some things are so obvious that we go through. Those deep things that no one really wants to talk about or get into. Yet, it becomes our story where it works to help others.

By your storynot what we have that makes us beautiful (hair, face, clothing, weight) what makes us beautiful is our positive attitude. Even through the dark times we really push through. Not everybody can recover. In periods of brokenness it didn't destroy you.

"We are hard-pressed on every side, yet not crushed; we are perplexed, but not in despair; persecuted, but not forsaken; struck down, but not destroyed."

2 Corinthians 4:8-9

A lot of people go through situations and they never recover they don't bounce back. They are never the same again and not all is positive. If we are never the same again it should be for God's glory.

"But we all, with unveiled face, beholding as in a mirror the glory of the Lord, are being transformed into the same image from glory to glory, just as by the Spirit of the Lord."

2 Corinthians 3:18

So many deep trials that people go through and many just don't recover.

What now becomes a part of your story is how did you do it?

How did you survive? How did you get up? How did you smile?

How did you find the strength to even show up anywhere?

What were your thoughts?

For every level is a new devil, so we need to write it down, testify, use it as a manual, a learning tool in life should we experience other pressing and challenging situations.

How do I keep positive in the midst of turmoil?

How do I smile? How do I find beauty in brokenness?

How do I find who I am when I'm losing everything that seems to define me?

Those are things we can share powerful testimonies.

Even when it wasn't easy, through the night watches how did you overcome? Through that dark.

It's always about changing a mindset! I have to learn to change the way that I think of myself or about my situation. There is beauty in broken things. I love the definition of broken because it doesn't mean that you don't work. It just means that you are not functioning properly! You still function and the rest that is missing God places His grace over it. You are just reduced. Smaller and God does GREAT things with less!!! A lot of those things happen so we don't get so big of ourselves or think we can do it alone.

❖   past participle of break.

❖   reduced to fragments; fragmented.

❖   ruptured; torn; fractured.

❖   Not functioning properly; out of working order.

When you turn it around I am a survivor! I am not

offended! I am going to move on. We become so victorious.

We all have a unique story worth sharing. Tell the world! Facebook, IG, Twitterwrite a blog; a book; create a video! It's so worth it! We have to learn when we go through it.

Still smiling, laughing. When you went through the break up, the sickness, the darkness and all the loss.

Those things we do through it, that make us such a powerful person IN GOD!

There is always a moment we all have where we thought we were going to lose it!

Can't emphasize enough how we respond to pure pain, emptiness, treatment, loss can be so mind blowing.

Remembering those dark moments, you realize that in those times you can't really help someone. We wish we can remove the pain for us and even for others. But we go through it. Through many agonizing times, but it does and serves its purpose. It's our tool, our fuel – it is what God is going to use. Our thorn. It doesn't matter what the thorn isa thorn is a thorn and we all have them. Sad in itself but that it makes one so powerful in God.

"Concerning this thing I pleaded with the Lord three times that it might depart from me. And He said to me, "My grace is sufficient for you, for My strength is made perfect in weakness." Therefore most gladly I will rather boast in my infirmities, that the power of Christ may rest upon me." 2 Corinthians 12:8-9

Not only going through loss in some way other things can counterattack us to try to silence us. But we can speak up and confess that God is able to help us through. We cancel out the seeds that the enemy tries to sow and allow God's seeds of hope to grow!

We will be a witness! We will testify! We can share! We can explain! We can uplift! We can get through this! Because of our chains it advances the gospel.

We have risen above adversity.

We all have a story.

17 Chapters to provide some inspiration as the year of 2017 came to conclusion. It truly was a year of total victory because we chose to rise above adversity.

Now as we face the next year we find ourselves in another adverse situation. This one we never saw coming. These things happen from one day to the next. But our family will fight through it. May the generals of our faith continue to rise through adversity.

Juan Mendez

Nelly Montalvo

Mina Rivera

Cristina Mendez

I honor your faith and perseverance. You finished the year strong and started this one steadfast! This book is our family lifeline. It is our declaration that brought us into our destiny.

WE WILL RISE!
Love you.

"By Your spirit I will rise
From the ashes of defeat
The resurrected King, is resurrecting me
In Your name I come alive
To declare Your victory
The resurrected King, is resurrecting me"

– Resurrected King Lyrics by Elevation Worship

www.ingramcontent.com/pod-product-compliance
Lightning Source LLC
Chambersburg PA
CBHW030902170426
43193CB00009BA/713